T0193831

GOD IS NOT IN CONTROL

W.J. Fair

WESTBOW
P R E S S®
A DIVISION OF THOMAS NELSON
& ZONDERVAN

WestBow Press books may be ordered through booksellers or by contacting:

WestBow Press
A Division of Thomas Nelson & Zondervan
1663 Liberty Drive
Bloomington, IN 47403
www.westbowpress.com
1 (866) 928-1240

ISBN: 978-1-9736-5824-5 (sc)
ISBN: 978-1-9736-5825-2 (e)

Print information available on the last page.

WestBow Press rev. date: 03/27/2019

Before you start to read this book, pray that God will give an open heart and mind. If you already have an opinion of what you are going to read, then you will miss the big picture.

I believe this book is a way to start, increase and understand what God has in store for you. God loves you and wants the best for you.

This book is also for me. I have gone through a lot in my short life. Writing this book and studying the Bible and reading other books has opened my eyes to a lot of things I have done wrong and could be doing better.

By purchasing this book, then maybe you are looking for answers. If you are reading this, then I have peaked your interest. Either way, this book will give answers and raise questions in your own heart, as it has done mine.

If things offend you as you read this book, then that maybe a way of God telling you that this is an area of life you need to look at. Remember through all this, God loves you. Until you can realize and understand this, life will knock you down. I thank you for your interest in this book and look forward to seeing you grow.

Hopefully the title of this book has peaked your interest. What is this guy talking about? How can he say that? Well, as you read this book, maybe I will answer that question.

Some of what you read is my belief and understanding of the Bible. I write with an open mind and heart. You may not agree with all that you read, but I have my convictions and beliefs. God has put this book on my heart to write and I believe this book will help others grow and become stronger in their spiritual life.

This book is not written to make you change your belief system or your convictions. I hope through reading this book, you can change your vocabulary to start thinking the way God needs you to think to become closer to Him and be able to let Him use you for the purpose He has designed you for.

Over the beginning of the new century, we have seen a lot of destruction of America and we are at war with a lot of people and countries. My belief is that God has taken His hand off America. Not because He has abanded us, but because we have abanded Him. Not all things have been bad, but for the most part is our fault as Christians not standing up for our beliefs and convictions. If we as Christians want the world to change, we need to start in our own communities and cities first. We need to stand up and be bold for Christ. (II Tim 1:7) We need to not be ashamed of who we are as Christians (II Tim 1:8) and speak the truth. Life will give you problems, but knowing who is in control and who is in charge will make the difference in the outcome.

God has a purpose and plan for each of us. We need to be able to use words that increase our faith, not just filler words.

We need to change our words that inspire people, not just make them feel better. Our words can tear people down, but the right words will lift people up and encourage them.

Now don't get me wrong. God is God and can do what He wants, when He wants (Daniel 4:35). But because of His love, mercy and grace, He chooses not to. He gave us free will and is willing to let us make our own decisions.

God is not in control but He is in charge. I know to some this is just a play on words. But if as Christians we want to be more Christ like, we need to change our thinking and choose the right words. It is no longer our mind set, but the mindset of Christ. As lawyers, judges, bosses, teachers should choose their words to get their points across, so do we as Christians need to. Our lives are to be a reflection of Christ, as well as our words. Anybody who wants to see their ideas brought to actions have to use the right words to make sure the product is the same as the idea.

I have not been able to find any definition of "in control" or "in charge" in any dictionary. These may not be the proper meanings, but we can discuss that later if you want.

The phrases are used for the purpose of this book and to help start a change in the way you think and talk. This book is to be used to grow closer to God, not something to argue about.

I know this is just a matter of word play or semantics, but we need to change our words to change our thinking to change our blessings.

This comes down to the "can I –may I " debate. The first is asking someone if they think you have the aptitude or skills to complete a task. The second is asking permission to do something you know you have the skills to complete.

If we don't change the way we talk to God, then we will not get the things we need. Saying "I would really like a new car" is different than "God, if it is in your will, I am asking for the means for a new vehicle that will fit into my budget." Now you should have the budget working first. God is not going to give you something you cannot handle.

Let me try to put this in a different light. The owner of a company is in control of the whole company and has the authority to do as they wish. The GM has the authority to do the same because it was given to him or her by the owner. That is the extent of being in charge.

To be in control, the GM asked people to do a task and because they need a job, they do it. The only problem is how the people complete the task. The job is done and done correctly, but not in the manner or way the GM would have done it. That is a loss of control. You can tell people how to do something (in charge), but you cannot get them to do the task the same way you would do it (loss of control), even though the results are the same.

Let's look at this another way. As a parent, you want your children to do well. God has put you in charge of them. You can tell your children to do something, but you cannot control the way they do it. Every person is different and we all do things differently.

God understands this and still gave us free will. God has the angels as yes men. He wanted someone to have a relationship with and can have conversations with people and their own ideas and thoughts.

God has the power to control, but because of free will, He gives us the right to choose. We can choose to do what pleases us or do what is pleasing to God. I have done both and have realized that pleasing God is much more rewarding than doing what I want.

I know there a lot of people who believe God is in control, but by the definition, we must be willing to let God lead, guide or direct us. All things must go through God first.

In the Old Testament, there are several verses that say God is in control. Let's look at Job. Satan went before God and said that if God would destroy everything Job has, Job would curse God. (Job 1:11). God let satan do to Job what he wanted to do, except kill Job. This is one way God is in charge but not in control. Satan had to come before God to ask permission (God in control), but could do to Job what he wanted (God in charge).

In Genesis 1:28, God gave Adam dominion over the earth. Dominion, as defined by the Bible dictionary is, "Power or Right of governing and controlling with sovereign authority." In other words, Adam had control over the earth. Control in this sense was to rule with power and jurisdiction. After Adam and Eve sinned, Adam loss dominion over the earth and satan became in control. By this, satan became in charge, as being the one who had command, rule and manipulation of the earth. Two different types of control, but the second one only has charge of the earth.

As you go through the Old Testament, God is in control and in charge of a lot of situations. This was to get to the destination of the birth of Christ.

When the Israelites were in Egypt and Moses was trying to get them out, God was in charge and control of the plagues, but not in control of pharaoh's decisions of not letting the Israelites go. God did persuade pharaoh's answers through the plagues.

In the Old Testament, people were under the law of the Ten Commandments. These were the rules for all Israelites. The Old Testament was for the direction of the Jews, again get to the destination of Christ. They were giving directions of how to get to the promise land, but because of free will and sin, choose to be ungrateful and never make it to the promise land.

God had to control people in the Old Testament to push people. A short trip did not have to last 40 years. BUT, because people were not willing to listen to and follow God their journey became one of heartache, trials and disappointment.

Everybody had to go through a high priest to go to God. After Christ died on the cross we have a direct link to God. This is the relationship God wants with us, just like He had with Adam in the beginning.

I know some people are saying that I can control my children. I tell them do something or there will be consequences. Or some bosses telling their employees what to do or they will be fired.

That is not control, that is manipulation which takes away free will. As a person who has been in the worker and boss positions, I have learned how to deal with people from both sides.

God gave us free will and will not manipulate us to do His will. He has rewards in the form of blessings for us. He wants our obedience and rewards our obedience but He will not tell us our blessings ahead of time.

He wants you to do it out of obedience and not because of the rewards. He will discipline us when we sin but will not take things away from us because we don't act the way we should. He is the business of reaching people and loving people. God wants people to come to Him, not be afraid of Him. He knew we would fall, but always wanted the relationship of love with us.

People have to learn to trust God. This is the only way to have a relationship with Him. Life can be very difficult and with no one in charge and telling us how to act, it will only get worse.

God is in charge and if we follow His directions and do it according to His directions, life will get easier. People want something or someone to point them in the right direction. Those who are in charge have a greater responsibility to those who look to them for guidance. Just because you are the one who is supposed to be in charge doesn't mean you have no one to answer to.

Your responsibility as an owner of a company is not only to your customers, but also to your employees. You have to be a strong, transparent, fair and faithful leader. If you don't believe in the company's mission, then you will have problems getting people to follow you.

The same is for the lead pastor of a church. If you don't show you have a passion for the mission of God, reaching and loving people, then you will never get people to believe in it either.

I am just trying to get you to believe that God loves you and has your life in His hands, if you are willing to let Him have control of it. It is just up to you to decide how much stays in His hands. If you are willing to let God have control, then He will help you through life.

I know people who are wondering why certain things happen to good people? These are to test some people to strengthen their faith and some are for others to see if God can truly use them. Sometimes God knows they have suffered enough, or have more suffering ahead and calls them home. People make promises to God and say they will do things for Him if He ever asks, but when it comes they back out. God will trust you with small things first before He will trust you with greater things.

Now those people who are not Christians and ask God for help will be surprised by what is next. This may also surprise some Christians. The answer is, you are not part of His family. In John 17:9, Jesus didn't pray for those not in God's family. The only thing God hears from non-Christians is the prayer of salvation.

He cannot help those who are not part of His family. Don't hear what I am not saying. When someone who is a Christian prays for a non-Christian, God will hear you. Your prayer is heard and if it will turn someone towards God, He will answer the prayer according to His will.

God looks at the heart and how He can use you or the person you are praying for. God does answer prayers.

How can you help others that are not in your family? You watch for kids and try to help keep them out of harm, if you care, but I will not take care of somebody else's kid while mine suffers. You have to take care of your own first. That is what God does; He takes care of His children first.

Remember Job, satan had to ask God first. That is the way it is today. God is in charge and satan has to ask permission first. This doesn't mean you will not be tempted by satan, just he has to get permission to do you harm. The way you respond to temptation, is how it will be determined if you are harmed or not. You may have trials, but let God be in control and enjoy the ride.

God loves us and wants the best for us. He wants to have control, but He sits back and lets us make our own mistakes. That is how we mature and grow.

If God did everything for us, we would never appreciate it. God had plans for greatness for us, but sin came into the world through Adam and Eve. Once kicked out of Eden, I can almost guarantee they realized how great they had it and learned to appreciate everything they had after that.

We have to realize the same thing. If everything is given to us without a price, then we never realize the sacrifice people and God go through to supply us our needs.

The greatest price was Christ dying on the cross and the greatest sacrifice was God having to turn away because of sin. I believe we as Christians lose sight of this.

We always look at the open tomb and the power of God, but forget the love of God on the cross. It is that love that will help us stay calm in times of crisis. It is the power that helps us through those crises.

God is always there and will never leave us. It is sin that keeps us from God. Our pride will keep us from seeking God and His guidance. It is our pride that will keep us from asking for forgiveness. It is our pride that will keep us from helping others. It is our pride that will cloud our outlook on life and wonder where God is.

Letting go of pride will clear up our vision of God and people. We will see others as God sees them, as important people Christ died for.

God does see people differently than we can. He sees His children through glasses covered with Christ's blood. We don't have this luxury, but we can have the same heart as Christ.

People are important and they all have the same chance to accept Christ. Let God be in control of saving them and learn to try to lead people to Him.

As Christians, we have to fall "IN LOVE" with God. When you love someone, you do things for them wanting something back in return. When you are "IN LOVE" with someone one, you do things for them without expecting anything in return. God is "IN LOVE" with us. His love is unconditional. He is patient enough to wait on us to return His love by showing it. We have to show Him we love Him because He knows our hearts.

He wants us to show Him because words are empty. Actions speak louder than words, as we have heard all our lives. God knows that if we spend time with Him, we will grow and be able to show His love to others.

Being "IN LOVE" with someone means just spending time with them. Now with people it is just sitting in the same room and watching TV. Or being next to each other just holding hands. Being in the same room just being able to see each other. You do for each other just because you love them.

Unless you have never been "IN LOVE" you will never understand this. Now do not get me wrong. Relationships have their ups and downs, but people "IN LOVE" stay in love. This is because in the end they both know they cannot make it without each other.

Now this is the relationship we need to have with God. No matter what is going on in our lives, we need to ask ourselves, "Is God enough?" By this I mean with all that I am going through, if I lose everything, can I make it with just God and His provisions?

This is what Job did. He knew God was the only one to help make it through. Yes, it is nice to have people around us to get through the tough times, but is God Enough?

People come and go in our lives, but God never changes. We hate to see people leave our lives that we have come to love. It hurts to lose friends or have to move, but God is the one moving us even if we are not the ones physically moving. He wants to know if He is enough.

This is the part where we have to let God have control. If He is enough for you, then you will trust Him with everything and let Him have control.

Now this is the part that is hard. I had a hard time with it. I was coming home from work one night and told God I was tired. I was tired of fighting with my wife.

Tired of working long hours and having nothing to show for it. Tired of just being tired.

So, I gave it to God and felt a little relief. But something just didn't feel right. I was still struggling financially. My wife and I were still fighting. What was going on? I was thinking, maybe it takes a little while.

This went on for about two years and I was getting tired again. I asked God, "I gave it all to you, why hasn't life changed?" His reply, "You gave it to Me, but you never LET GO!"

I wanted God to have control of my life, but I wasn't willing to let go of the control.

Until I was willing to let go of the control, God could not bless me the way He had things in store for me.

I still struggle to let go, but have learned that if I let God work, the end results are way better than I could have imagined. Most of the time the situations get resolved faster and less stressful also.

I get a real kick out of how many preachers and religious sights say God is in control. As I have tried to find references of God being in control, the only place that the Bible says God had control over something is in Revelations 16:9.

The other references that have to do with control, is self-control. So, that tells me we have to have self-control. That tells me God is only in control of what we, self, give to Him.

I am not trying to knock preachers that teach this way, even though it seems that way. I am telling everybody to change your speech and thoughts on the control of God. If we continue to believe God is in control, then we lose sight of His power and just continue to do as we want, because it will all work out. Remember the saying, "Faith without works is dead"? This is how to weaken your faith by telling yourself God is in control. You want God to do His part but are not willing to do your part. Your part is prayer, reading His word for answers and believing the answers you receive.

God doesn't want us to be confused on what He has for us. He wants us to be able to come to Him without the fear of Him being a mean God. He loves us and wants the best for us. We still have to show Him the reverent fear of Him being God, just don't be fearful that He is out to get you.

You have to have a love relationship with God. A true love relationship is a give - give relationship. When you love with someone, you do things for them not expecting anything in return. When you love someone, you trust that what they say, they will do.

The same must go for a relationship with God. God will bless you if you are obedient to Him and His word. I don't tithe just expecting to get something in return. I tithe out of loving God and trusting Him to do what His word says. I don't serve at church for personal recognition, but out of obedience and loving people.

It doesn't matter how good you think you are, or how pretty or handsome or how much you do. If you don't do it with God, then it is for self.

That empty feeling you get after the rush of doing something the world thinks is great, is the missing of God. God sees your heart; the world sees you. Don't do things to out of wanting to belong or make people proud of you. Do things to glorify God. He is proud of you as His child and He will lift you up.

God's plan will continue, even when we become stubborn and refuse to do what He asks us to do. He will find someone else to do His will and will bless that person, we miss out on that blessing.

Blessing someone not only makes that person feel better, but humbles us to the love of God.

We need to quit being people of head knowledge and trying to show people look what I did. We need to become people with a heart knowledge of God and show people what God can do for them.

With letting God have control, we can start to let go of the past, live in the present and look forward to the future.

The only one who wants you to remember your past is satan. This is because he doesn't know your future and if he can keep you feeling bad about yourself, he can keep you from doing God's will.

God helps you forget you past, because He knows your future and the plans He has in store for you.

God doesn't look at your past when you become a Christian. He looks at the purpose for what He made you for and where He can lead you if you let Him have control. He wants to start with where you are, not where you were.

Accepting Jesus as your Savior is not to be used as a get out of hell card. If that is the reason you do it, then it was a head decision and not a heart decision.

Jesus loves you, but He wants to not only let Him be your Savior, but your leader and controller of your life.

But I don't want someone controlling me. Ok, then do it your way, have a hard time in life, then come back and realize that if I let God have control of my life, it would have turned out differently and better. Pride comes first, then disobedience of God, then the fall from God's grace all because you wanted to do it your way. Luke 15:11-24 talks of the Prodigal son. This is how we are and we finally realize that in God's will we are safe and we will be full spiritually.

Now there is the other part of the story in Luke 15:25-32 of the jealous brother. Basically, it says about those who do everything they think God wants them to do, but someone returns to God's family and the attention is taken off them. This is trying to tell us, don't feel left out. Someone has returned to God and the prayers of many have been answered. It is all about God and His love for us.

God designed us, He knows our needs, wants and desires. He knows our strengths and weaknesses. He knows our personalities and gave us all unique ones to use to further His Kingdom.

We all make mistakes in life, but if we continue to do the same thing over and over, then it has become a decision. We have to make good decisions in life, but if we ask God first, He will give us the answer, not only to better our lives, but also the ones around us. We have to plan our days, but if we start our day with God, He will make the day seem long enough to get all that we set out to do for that day done.

As we go through life, we seem to have times that are rougher than others. We also have times when the day just seems to go by effortlessly. Well, the times that are rough, if we look back, we will see we tried to do it on our own. The days that are good, we have let God control it.

Every time we try to control our days and situations, God is there but we forget to include Him and the project we are doing has problems. He has given us the best helper in the Holy Spirit, we sometimes forget to use Him.

Go back through the Old Testament in the Bible and you can see these same things happened to people in those books. As long as they went by God's directions (commandments), they had prosperous times. When they went against God's directions, they had hard times and failures. These are the differences between letting God have control and people trying to control themselves. As seen throughout the Bible, when God was in control, the Israelites had plenty and life was good for them.

This is how we must be. With God in control, our lives can be prosperous to the point of our lives being easier. I have had to learn this plenty of times through my life and career.

There have been times in my job as a diesel mechanic that the truck I was working on just came apart and went back together smoothly. There were other times that it seemed like everything I touched was either hard to come off or hard to go on.

Sometimes this was because I had gotten a big head and refused help or because I was trying to rush to finish. God has my life in control because I gave it to Him. The days that are hard was because I tried to take it back. The days that I tried to rush are the days He was trying to protect me.

The protection I saw later after I got frustrated on why something wasn't going back together good. I would finish the project and on the way home would go by an accident that I could have been involved in had the project finished on time.

Didn't God want to protect the people in the accident? I am sure He did, but maybe they were not in His family. Or maybe they had not let God have control of their lives. Don't know and refuse to speculate why He helped me and not them. All I know is He protects me, my family and all the things I have let Him have control of.

There is a guy that lives around us and is on a fixed budget. I see him going around trash cans to get extra money from cans. The other day I gave him some money just to bless him.

Just the other day I went to get gas and was talking to my wife about supper. We decided to have supper out that night. Well when I got to the pump, there was money taped to the pump. It was enough to pay for supper and give a tip to the person at the fast food place. Now we had the money to pay for it, just God blessing us for blessing others.

When you hear about people helping others and they get blessed, they are not bragging on "look what I did", they are bragging on God by saying, "Look what God can do if you obey Him."

The people who are bragging on themselves, you can tell because it will be all about them. The ones who are bragging on God, it will be all about HIM. God is the one who started the wheel in motion, so to speak, and will continue to push it along. It is up to us, if we are willing, to get on the roller coaster ride of life and determine how much we are going to enjoy the ride. God will be there when you, as His child, ask for help and direction in life.

But the ride is less bumpy when we ask before the curves and twist, than when we get in the middle. The end results are the same because God has already made the ride, but how we get through it, is on us.

As we learn to let God have control of our lives, we learn how much He loves us. The determining factor is not why He loves us, just that He loves us. We learn to trust Him more and learn life does get easier with Him ahead of us and beside us, instead of behind us to use when we see fit. He is behind us to catch us when we fall, but is so much better to have Him leads us and encourage us as we go through life.

As I sit here writing, I look back in life and realize how much He does love me. With the tragedies and disappointments, I have been through, I have learned, leaning on Him and trusting Him is the only way I have been able to get through them and move on with life. I have determined that I cannot let life dictate me, I dictate life. The only way I have been able to do this is let God have control. Sure, there are still times when life doesn't go as I have planned, but I realize that God has a bigger and better purpose for my life. So, when life gets me down, I have learned to lean on and trust Him more. There are times when satan puts thoughts into my head, but I have to laugh and remind him, that God has put me in the position I am in for His purpose and not mine. I have learned to ask for forgiveness during those times for not trusting God. I get reminded during those times that I have let God have control and He is working behind the scenes for my best interest and for His purpose. There are times that I still forget that and then things happen that make me look back and thank Him for getting me through.

I have learned to trust Him more and seek Him more. I get more understanding while reading His word. I learn more from hearing pastors teach. I have more peace about life in general. There are still bad days when I forget to trust. But the good days are starting to outweigh the bad days.

Letting God have control and letting go, has made life more abundant. Not just financially, as most people think, but physically, emotionally and mentally. He has given me answers when I am struggling to find them. He gives me words to say to help others not just spiritually but with customers. He also helps keep me calm when I want to tell people what I really think. He gives me the words to encourage people to want to better themselves. He gives me the words to say when praying for others. Life is just better!

There are times when I cannot sleep and I don't know why. But I am learning that these are times when He wants to talk with me and the house is quiet and we can talk. Sometimes, people are put on my mind and this is a quiet time to pray for them. I just know letting Him have control and learning to do His will, sometimes doesn't make sense, but life is so much better. He gives me rest when I do go back to sleep and makes it peaceful and I feel as I have slept for days. Just letting go and giving to God, has lifted such a burden off me that I feel calmer and more peaceful.

I am not saying everything in life has been great, but it gets better every day. I have learned how to love more and love differently. I have learned how to see people as ones that needs His love just as much as I do. Things may not always go as we plan, but they do go as God has planned. The destination is still the same, just how long it takes us to get there is on us. The more we let Him have control and learn to listen to Him, the easier life will get.

We still have a purpose of reaching others for Him and growing His Kingdom, but having Him help us, is easier to do than trying on or own. We will never fulfill our purpose He has set for us doing it on our own.

He has to have control. He has to be in charge. He is the only strength we have to continue. It is His love, grace and mercy that continues for us that keeps us wanting more of Him. It is His love that keeps us striving to do more for Him. Without His love, we can do nothing. We cannot love, pray, serve or give without loving Him back. He has to be our strength, our guide, our king and our Lord. The main reason people don't trust God is not a LACK of Faith; but an EXCESS of PRIDE. We need to take the pride binders off and see that God is there beside us to not only help us, but to lead, guide and direct us. With the binders on, we only see what is in front of us on the path we have chosen. If we take off the binders, we would see the path He has set for us and is willing to guide us, if we let Him have control and choose His path.

HE <u>MUST</u> HAVE CONTROL.

Now after reading all of that, you may still be wondering, "How do I let God have control"? Well you need to change. Without change, there is no growth. Without growth, you remain stagnant and will never see change. It is a vicious circle.

Next, the first thing you must do is have a relationship with Him. This is by accepting His Son as your Savior. If you have already done this, then you are heading in the right direction.

Next is to let the Holy Spirit be your guide. Fighting with the Holy Spirit is not letting God have control. The Holy Spirit is that still small voice in your head that is nudging you when you are doing something out of God's will. It is also that still small voice that will tell you that God has the situation you are in and let Him have it.

Next is FAITH. Without faith, it is impossible to do anything. If you don't have faith, not just in God, but yourself, you are setting yourself up for failure. That may sound harsh, but it is the truth. If you don't believe, lack of faith, that you cannot do something, then you won't.

Same goes for faith in God. If you don't believe He can do it, He won't.

The hardest part of letting God have control, is the lack of faith. Trusting God with all of your life, is hard. But not letting Him have control, makes life harder. You have to trust Him. He has our best interest in mind.

The next step is to start small, unless your faith is strong. Start with your finances, this will be the hardest part to let God have control of anyway. Start tithing off your net. But I struggle with 100% of my net, how am I going to get by on 90%? Trust God and let Him work. Malachi 3:10 says to bring ALL the tithes into the storehouse. At that time, it wasn't just money, but grains, fruit, food so to speak. The store house was to help the less fortunate. I not saying we just give everything we have away, but give your 10% of your pay, and when you are out grocery shopping, pick up a couple of extra items, if you can afford it, for your church's food pantry.

When I said if you can afford it, I meant, if you are just starting to tithe, let God bless you first for being obedient, then as the blessings get bigger and you can then afford to bless others.

Now that God is blessing you for being obedient in tithing and you understand why, try giving God control of your kids. This was a hard one for me also. My son when he was smaller, he was tested for ADHD. But during the testing we found out he was borderline for Ash Berger.

So, I had to let God have control of this. As a parent, we want our children to be healthy, but God gives us things in our children to help our faith grow. My son still has some symptoms of this but he is getting better and he is changing as he learns to trust God more.

But trusting God with our children is going to be hard. We see them hurt, love, hate, smile and grow. They may be our children here on earth, but they were given to us by God to nurture, inspire and teach about him. We can't make all the decisions for them, but letting God have control over them as far as being safe while not with us, (i.e. school, sports, dates, out with friends), is a battle. Satan will put thoughts in your head when they don't answer their phone or a text, as what are they doing, are they ok, where are they at? Some of this is being a parent and setting boundaries, the other part is satan trying to get you to doubt God. By letting God have control over them, you can tell satan to get behind you because they are in God's hand and satan can't hurt them.

As a parent we shouldn't be loyal to a church or preacher. If your child is not learning to the point where they are growing spiritually, then as a parent you need to find out why. If the student pastor isn't teaching the Word of God and just making the students feel good, then time to find a new leader or a new church. If your student is no longer excited about going church, then there is a problem. Our job as a parent is to raise them according to God's word and help them grow so when they leave,

God goes with them. You give God control over them and raise them His way. After they leave for life, you pray that God will protect them and pray that they make good and correct decisions in life through God. We are to love our children as God loves us. They will frustrate us, upset us and will become disappointed in them at times, but those are no reasons to stop loving them. God does that to us as His children. We are to encourage and support them. Not in things against God's will, but things that they accomplish and are important to them. They will always be a part of our lives and hopefully they will always comeback to us for advice. If we, as parents, do our job according to God's word, they will always want to come back to visit.

We cannot do this with God though. He must be who we go to before making decisions. He is the one with all the answers, the correct answers.

Next, let God have control of your job. If you are looking for work, ask God to open doors so you can get a job that will let you be used with the skills and talents you have, to not only make you get better, but help better the company. Ask for a job where you can be used by Him, to further His Kingdom. If you have a job, but are not sure why you are there, ask God to show you why and how you can be used by Him.

We must get out of the mindset of what can I get out of this and into the mindset of how can God be shown thru this. How can God use me to further and grow His

Kingdom in the job I am in? Sometimes we are put in a position, with a platform, to be used by God. Sometimes we are in a position just to be around people that need Him or they have questions about God and He is setting you up to help others. He will give you the words to say to people, if you ask Him to, but be ready to be amazed by what comes out of your mouth, because it is the Holy Spirit talking, not you.

The next area of life is your marriage. If both you and your spouse are Christians, then both of you need to do this. If only one of you is a Christian, then you need to ask God to show His love for the other thru you. Don't ask God to change them, ask God to change you. God will convict the other, by you loving the other and you standing on your faith and doing what God wants you to do.

The next one is going to shock some of you, as it did me. You must let God have control of YOU. What do I mean? I am a Christian, so doesn't that mean God has control of me? NO! As a Christian, we are part of God's family, but because of free will, we still do what we want to do. Letting God have control of you, means you strive every day, in everything you do, to do His will. You become more obedient every day, to do what He wants and not what you want.

Life becoming stressful? Have you been doing what God wants or what you thought was best? Have you been doing His will for your life or just going through the motions? This list can go on and on. Letting God have control of you, is just that. You ask before you do. You get permission first, instead of doing then asking for forgiveness. Is He going to let you go and do your own thing? Yes, if that is what you choose to do. But by doing it your way, the blessings become less and life starts to get you down. Then it effects your marriage, your relationship with your kids and relationships with others.

This has become your choice. God will help you, but you have to make the choice of who you are going to trust every day. God or yourself? Choosing ourselves makes life harder and less fulfilling. Choosing God, makes life easier, (more abundant), and relationships grow closer.

We have to determine if our morals are better than God's word. Our morals CANNOT determine our lives. Just because my morals don't match yours, doesn't make me wrong and vice versa. If we all get back to God's morals, then there will be less fighting among Christians. People are no longer worried about right and wrong. They argue over whose morals are right or wrong. As God's children, we need to help others realize that God's ways are the best ways to prosper, enjoy life and live happier.

I have some relationships that have been broken up because of my selfishness and wanting something out of it the other person didn't want to give up. I have relationships where I don't see people every day or talk to them every day, but when we get together, we just pick up like we just saw each other the previous day. But I have relationships that get stronger every day because I let God have control of them and look for ways to make their lives better.

The relationships where I look out for others and not what I can get out of it, are the ones that God blesses me. This is just not on a personal basis, but also on a work basis. I try to have a relationship with those I work with, for or under my supervision. I want to see these people succeed. This also goes for my customers, as I try to develop a relationship to where they see I have their best interests in mind without hurting the company I work for.

As you go along, trusting God, not only does it become easier to let Him have control, but it makes life easier. Will this be an overnight success? No, but with faith and time it will become a need in your life. It will be how you start your day, by asking God to have control and ending your day by praising Him for the successes in your day. It will be something that you begin to realize you forgot to ask in the beginning of your day and you stop and ask Him to have control of the rest of your day. It becomes what you need in your day. You will see relationships grow stronger and better. You will develop a mindset of how can I help others, how can God's love shine through this? It will become where you look forward to the day and wonder how God is going to use you. It becomes a joy just to be living. It becomes to where you worry less and smile more, become stronger in your faith, praises come on a moment by moment basis. Life just gets better.

Hopefully by reading this, you have a better understanding of God's love for you. You will begin to increase your faith and start to enjoy life more. Remember joy comes from the Lord and that is not something that can be taken away, only given up.

The choice is yours and I hope this book will help you make the choice to live life according to God's will and not our own. Take time to read His word and look to it for lives answers. They are in there. It is just a choice of do I want to grow and get out of the pit I am in or do I want to stay in my own self-pity? Life doesn't have to be that hard. It is up to each individual to make their own choices and learn to trust God and let life get better or do it our way and struggle.

I pray that whoever gets this book and applies these things to their life, will be blessed and grow in their faith. It is up to us as Christians to make those around us feel loved, and to encourage each other to be better for God's purpose.

Thank you,

With Love in Christ.

.

Printed in the United States
By Bookmasters